I am DEFINITELY, PROBABLY ENOUGH (I THINK)

REVELATIONS ON THE JOURNEY TO SELF-LOVE

TORI PRESS

CREATOR OF revelatori

ADAMS MEDIA
New York London Toronto Sydney New Delhi

Adams Media
An Imprint of Simon & Schuster, Inc.
57 Littlefield Street
Avon, Massachusetts 02322

Copyright © 2020 by Tori Press.

All rights reserved, including the right to reproduce this book or portions thereof in any form whatsoever. For information address Adams Media Subsidiary Rights Department, 1230 Avenue of the Americas, New York, NY 10020.

First Adams Media hardcover edition May 2020

ADAMS MEDIA and colophon are trademarks of Simon & Schuster.

For information about special discounts for bulk purchases, please contact Simon & Schuster Special Sales at 1-866-506-1949 or business@simonandschuster.com.

The Simon & Schuster Speakers Bureau can bring authors to your live event. For more information or to book an event contact the Simon & Schuster Speakers Bureau at 1-866-248-3049 or visit our website at www.simonspeakers.com.

Interior layout by Sylvia McArdle
Illustrations by Tori Press

Manufactured in China

10 9 8 7 6 5 4 3 2 1

ISBN 978-1-5072-1290-5
ISBN 978-1-5072-1291-2 (ebook)

For DAVID

WHO Sees AND LoVeS me
as I really am

AND WHo TeaCHeS me
To Do THe Same.

ONCE UPON a TIME, THERE LIVED a POWERFUL, magICAL, WONDROUS, aSTOUNDING BEING of LIMITLESS POTENTIAL

IN OTHER WORDS, SHE WAS AN

ORDINARY HUMAN

FOR WE ARE ALL OF US MAGICAL, AND WONDROUS, AND IMBUED WITH OUR OWN UNIQUE AND POWERFUL POTENTIAL, WHETHER WE REALIZE IT OR NOT.

LIKE aLL HumanS,
SHe was IMPERFECT.

PARKING TICKET
CITY OF LOS ANGELES

$80

SHe made
MISTaKeS

SHe SHoWed
POOR
JUDGMENT

Sure, I'LL HaVe
ANoTHer COCKTaiL!

SHE HATED HER
HAIR,
HER SKIN,
HER TEMPER,
HER
PERSONALITY,
HERSELF.

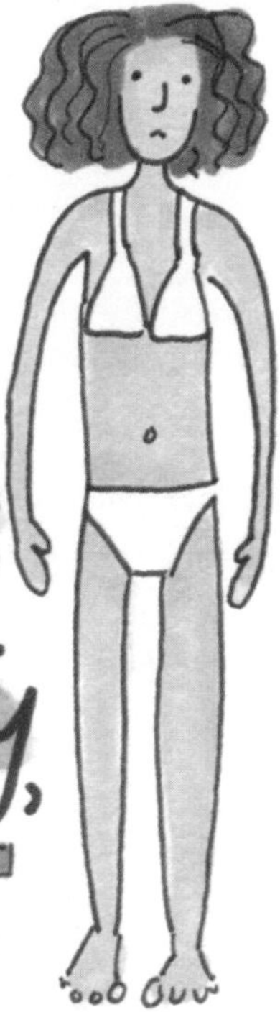

HER MIND WAS USUALLY TANGLED INTO A BIG KNOT OF ANXIETY

AND SOMETIMES SHE WOULD DISAPPEAR INTO DARKNESS

NONE OF THAT CHANGED WHO SHE WAS

BUT SHE BELIEVED IT DID.

WHERE SHE MIGHT HAVE SEEN
HER OWN VIBRANCE
& CHARM, HER UNIQUE
BRAND OF MAGIC

passionate ✳ Loyal BRave
KIND curious
creative WORTHY
(J J)

SHE SAW ONLY HER **IMPERFECTIONS**, HER INADEQUACIES, HER **SHORTCOMINGS**.

FRIZZY HAIR
(ALSO GOING GRAY)

TALKS TOO MUCH

IMPATIENT

SLOW EMAIL RESPONDER

YELLER

A LITTLE EXTRA.

SHE COULD NOT SEE THE TRUTH OF HERSELF BECAUSE SHE TOLD HERSELF a STORY.

you are NOT enough

THIS STORY.

THE STORY HAD MANY DIFFERENT VERSIONS

STOP BEING SO ANXIOUS

YOU SUCK

WHAT'S WRONG WITH YOU

YOU ARE SO WEIRD AND AWKWARD

YOU LOOK AWFUL

YOU'RE DISAPPOINTING EVERYONE

YOU'RE AN IMPOSTOR

YOU'RE A FAILURE

IT WAS AS FAMILIAR TO HER AS HER OWN FACE

BUT IT WAS STILL JUST a STORY

Harry Potter
1984
You are NOT ENOUGH
To Kill a Mockingbird
FAIRY TALES
LORD OF THE RINGS

POPULAR FICTION

AND a STORY IS NOT aLways True

IT DOESN'T HAVE TO BE **BELIEVED.** IT CAN BE CHANGED.

you are ~~NOT~~ enough

AND, THOUGH CHANGING a STORY IS LONG, ARDUOUS WORK— LIFE'S WORK—

SHE THOUGHT THAT MAYBE SHE WOULD TRY TO CHANGE HERS

I WISH I COULD say THAT THIS IS a NEAT AND TIDY STORY WITH a NEAT AND TIDY BEGINNING, MIDDLE, & END.

IT'S NOT. IT'S MESSIER THAN THAT—BECAUSE IT'S a REAL STORY, a HUMAN STORY. MY STORY.

I'M STILL SOMEWHERE ON THE **JOURNEY** TO BELIEVING I am ENOUGH— TO **SELF-LOVE**.

BUT I am HERE ON THE PaTH. I'M LEARNING TO See myself as I am— a magical, WONDROUS, **HUMAN** BEING

AND TO KNOW THAT I AM DEFINITELY, PROBABLY ENOUGH (I THINK)

STORIES I TELL MY-
SELF THE
MOST

(HISTORICAL)

Sorry... but you can't

it is just logic

you failed, therefore you're a failure

all of it

IT'S your fault

THE classic Bestseller

you're NOT good enough

STORIES I TELL MYSELF THE MOST

(RECENT)

OF more THAN you KNOW!

you are CAPABLE

you CAN HANDLE IT

IT'S okay To HAVE UPS and DOWNS

IT'S okay! REALLY!

mistakes are allowed

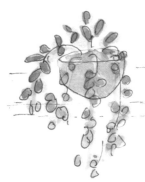

you are ENOUGH

FOR REAL, you are

ONE OF MY OLDEST AND MOST FAMILIAR STORIES GOES LIKE THIS:

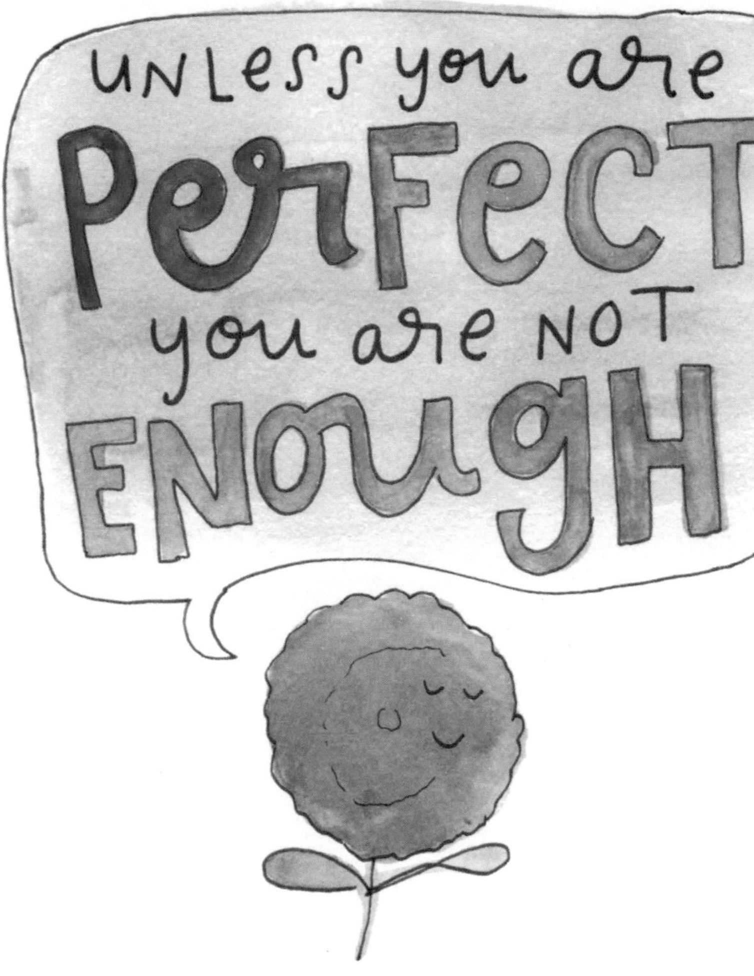
UNLESS you are
PERFECT,
you are NOT
ENOUGH

a MOTIVATOR
an ENCOURAGER

ace your exam!

make sure your
work is FLAWLESS!

INSPIRING me
TO DO my BEST

LATELY, THOUGH, INSTEAD OF expecting myself to be **PERFECT,** I've BEEN STRIVING FOR "**ISH.**"

"ISH" IS THE magical suffix THaT gives me some room To BReaTHe.

I keep my house clean.

ISH.

I eat a HEALTHY DIET.

ISH.

I PRACTICE SELF-care

meditation

exercise

you got THIS!

positive SELF-Talk

ISH.

STaying up way Too LaTe SCROLLING THROugH PosHMaRK

I'm going To BE SO TIRED Tomorrow BUT I CAN'T STOP

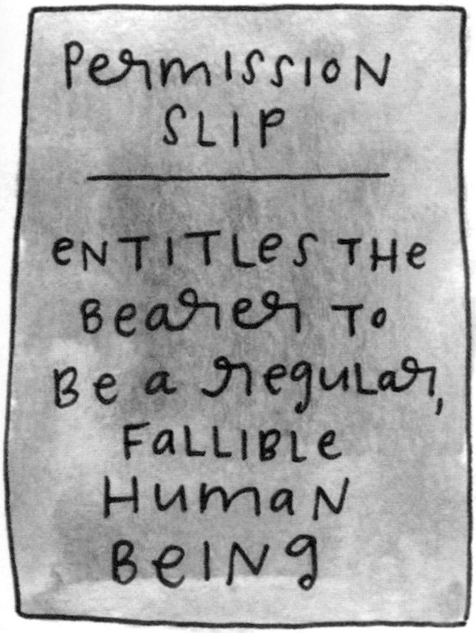

THE "ISH" gives me PERMISSION To Be Imperfect

THE "ISH" SAYS
IT'S OKAY TO HAVE
a BaD Day, TO
BaCKSLIDe, TO FaLL,
TO MISS THE MARK
AND TRY AGAIN.

IT SAYS I DON'T HAVE
TO BE PERFECT TO BE
OKAY, TO MAKE PROGRESS.

IT TELLS ME I CAN

BE HUMAN

AND GET IT WRONG

AND STILL BE

ENOUGH.

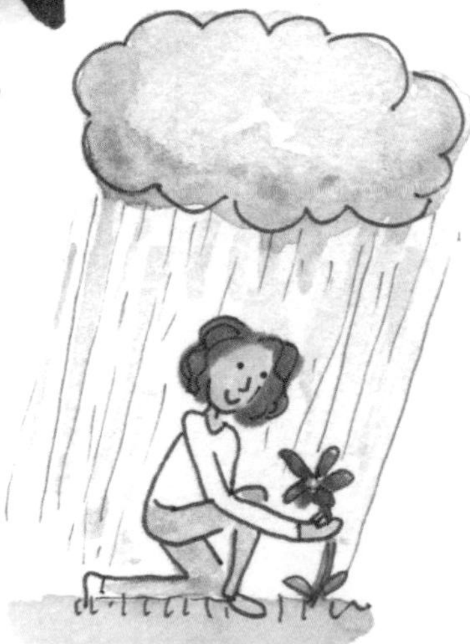

AND THAT'S SOME
PReTTY gOOD
ISH.

IF **HOW you are** DOING IN *Life* WERE a BELL CURVE, IT WOULD LOOK LIKE THIS:

WHERE you are MOST OF THE TIME

STRUGGLING

TOTALLY KILLING IT

BUT IF YOU ARE A *perfectionist*, TO YOU IT MIGHT LOOK MORE LIKE THIS:

This is, of course,

patently ridiculous.

Nobody on earth can constantly be the very best version of themselves.

Even Ruth Bader Ginsburg has her off days.

But not many.

AND IN FACT, HERE

IS WHERE you gain the WISDOM and EXPERIENCE you NEED to get HERE

EVERY LIFE

HAS ITS INEVITABLE HIGHS & LOWS. STRUGGLE IS A VITAL PART OF LIFE: A TEACHER, A FRIEND, A MIGHTY CATALYST FOR CHANGE. AND WHEN WE CAN STAY PRESENT WITH that TRUTH, THE BELL CURVE STOPS LOOKING LIKE THIS:

you COULD BE DOING BETTER

you're acceptable

aND STARTS
LooKiNg LiKe
THIS:

THE MENTAL Pressure Cooker

COOK UP AN EXISTENTIAL CRISIS!

INSTANT UNWANTED FEELINGS!

TONS OF USEFUL SETTINGS!

TRY IT IN IMPOSTOR SYNDROME MODE

FOR THE PRESSURE OF BELIEVING you're a FRAUD AND you DEFINITELY DON'T BELONG HERE

the EXPECTATIONS FEATURE

ADDS THE PRESSURE OF NEEDING THINGS TO GO A CERTAIN WAY

or PERFECTIONISM MODE

FOR THE PRESSURE OF TRYING TO LIVE UP TO IMPOSSIBLE STANDARDS

IN **OVERCOMMITTED** mode,

NEVER SAY NO! — AND ENJOY THE ~~TREMENDOUS PRESSURE~~ OF TOO MANY OBLIGATIONS

THE **PEOPLE PLEASING** FEATURE

a PERSONAL FAVORITE

THE PRESSURE OF RESPONSIBILITY FOR EVERYONE ELSE'S FEELINGS (WHILE your own go NEGLECTED)

GOOD VIBES ONLY mode

THE **PRESSURE'S ON** TO **ALWAYS** BE **POSITIVE**!!

EVEN IF YOU FEEL LIKE CRAP AND JUST WANT TO TAKE A NAP

SOUL-CRUSHING EFFECTS START INSTANTLY! GET ON THE FREEWAY TO FEELING BAD!

SHE SUCKS TO LIVE WITH.

BUT I CAN'T GET AWAY FROM HER

LIKE HAVING A TERRIBLE ROOMMATE, BUT FOR LIFE!

BECAUSE
SHE
IS
me.

BUT — AND
THIS IS THE
ImPORTANT
paRT ♥

She is NOT THE real me.

THE REAL ME IS THE ONE WHO NOTICES SHE'S TALKING

AND RESPONDS:

I've been hearing the voice of **ANXIETY** for as long as I can **remember,**

long before I knew what anxiety was

IT MANIFESTED ITSELF IN many ways as I grew up.

AS a KID, I MISSED SCHOOL ALL THE TIME BECAUSE MY OVERWHELMING ANXIETY made me FeeL SiCk.

IN HIGH SCHOOL AND COLLEGE, I MISSED **Hours** OF **Sleep** FOR THE same Reason.

BUT I STILL DIDN'T KNOW I was suffering from ANXIETY.

By the time I was in grad school, in my twenties, anxiety was hitting hard, with panic attacks, insomnia, nausea, even a

PUBLIC FAINTING EPISODE

at a university career fair

OH MY GOSH! IS SHE OKAY?

RESUME

FINALLY, aT almost 30, I saw a PSYCHIATRIST FOR THE FIRST TIME. SHE gave me a DIAGNOSIS OF

generalized anxiety DISORDER

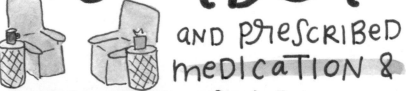

RX: TORI ZOLOFT

AND PRESCRIBED MEDICATION & THERAPY To HELP.

maybe these seem like small things:

a DIAGNOSIS,

miraculous medical technology to bring me back to myself,

therapy to help me see who I really am and change my story

BUT TOGETHER
THEY MADE
a PATH

a GENTLE TRAIL,
WINDING ITS SLOW, MEANDERING
WAY TOWARD HEALING.
TOWARD SELF-ACCEPTANCE.
TOWARD SELF-LOVE.

LIKE THERE IS AN ALARM GOING OFF IN MY HEAD ALL THE TIME

you are PROBABLY DOING SOMETHING WRONG!!!!

IT'S a JUNGLE IN HERE

IF ANXIETY IS MY CONSTANT
COMPANION, TELLING ME

you are NOTENOUGH

IN ITS URGENT VOICE FULL
OF TENSION AND FEAR AND
WORST-CASE SCENARIOS

THEN DEPRESSION
IS A SNEAKIER, SUBTLER, more
OCCASIONAL VISITOR

Depression slinks in during difficult times—like when I dropped out of grad school & didn't know what to do next

But it also slips in through the cracks, like smoke, in good times—times when I think I should be happy, like after I had my first baby

DEPRESSION DRAINS MY ENERGY. FEELS IMPOSSIBLE TO FIGHT

BUT MAYBE IT'S NOT MY JOB TO FIGHT IT.

MAYBE A FIGHT IS WHAT IT WANTS.

WHY ARE YOU HERE? WON'T YOU GO AWAY?

maybe my resistance gives it some of its power

but acceptance takes just a little bit of it away.

WHaT DoeS DePReSSION FeeL LIKe?

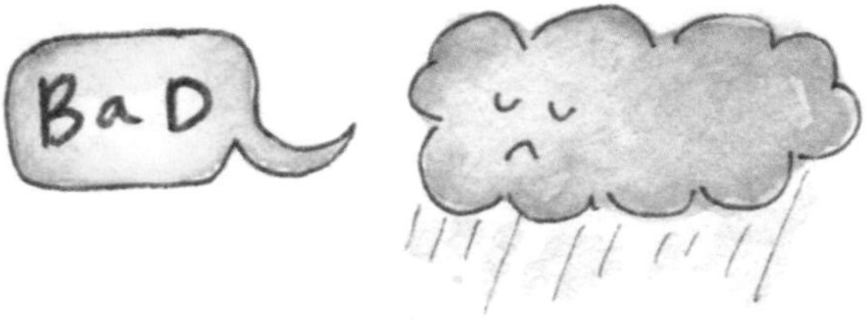

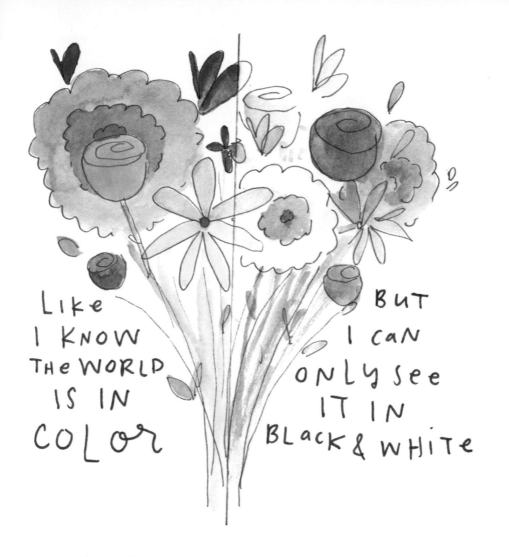

LIKE
I KNOW
THE WORLD
IS IN
COLOR

BUT
I CAN
ONLY SEE
IT IN
BLACK & WHITE

LIKE I am TOTally
DEPLETED & I LOST
my cHarger

LIKE THIS
IS all THERE
IS or WILL
ever BE

(IT ISN'T)

Like I am

aLONe

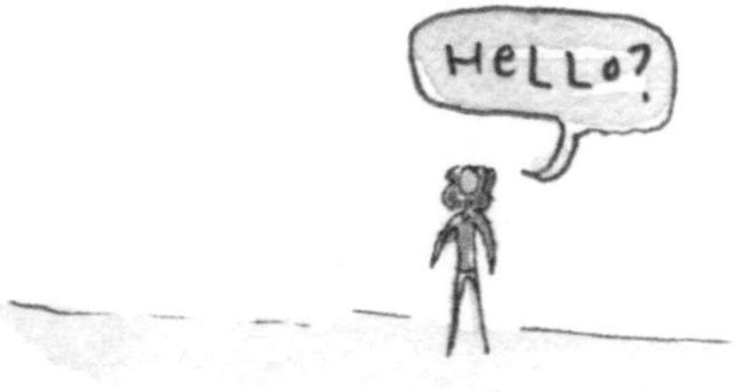

(I'm NOT)

LIKE IT'S FOREVER

(IT'S NOT!)

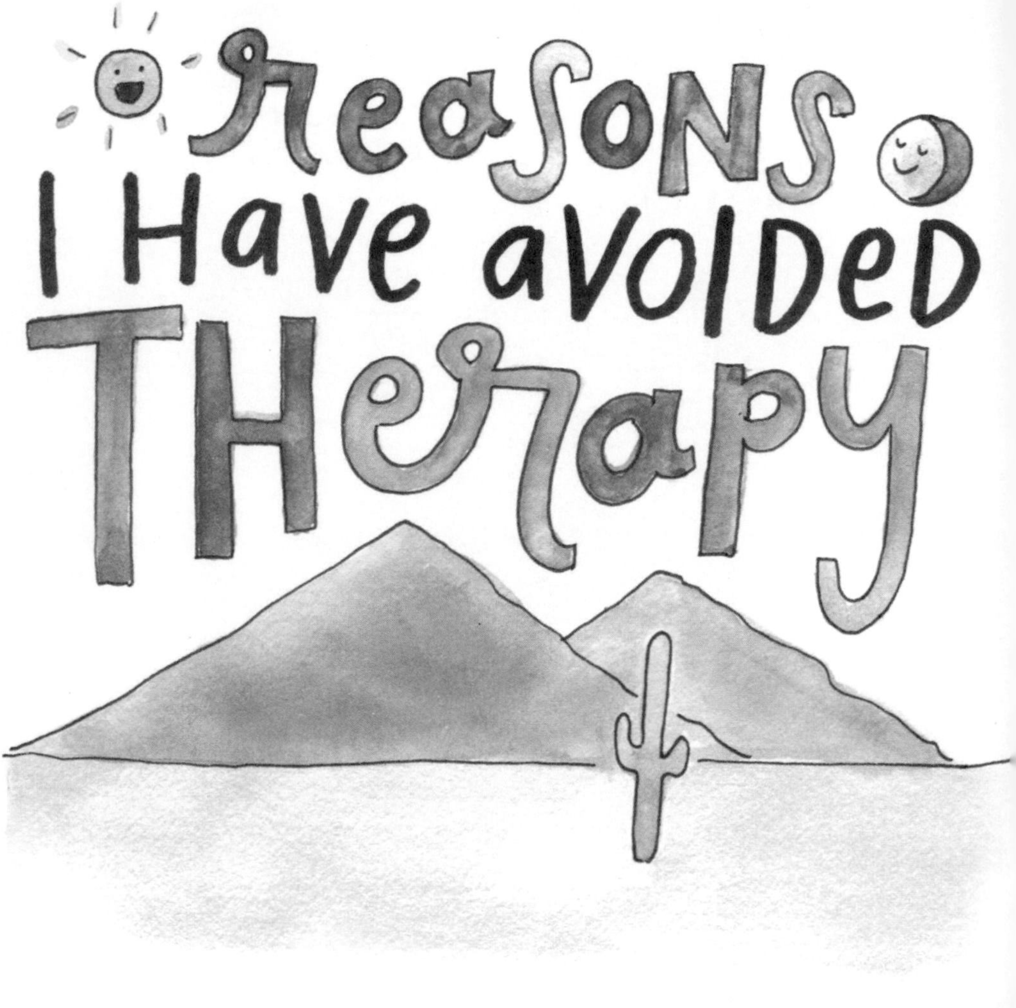
Reasons
I Have avoided
Therapy

I THINK maybe I can

get better on my own

* Sometimes these things really do help me!

Sometimes I need more.

WHAT IF THE THERAPIST
CONFIRMS
WOW YOU ARE LEGIT NUTS.
A HOPELESS CASE
ALL THE BAD THINGS
I THINK ABOUT MYSELF?

I've been before and it didn't WORK

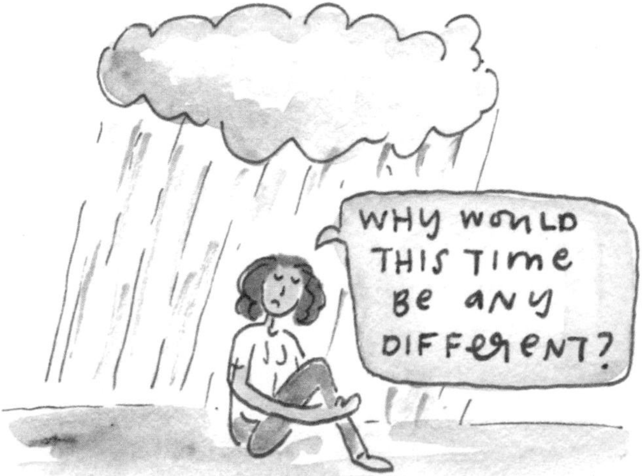

I'M JUST SCARED.

gulp

THERaPIST

THe reason I Have gone To THerapy:

WHAT HAPPENS IN THERAPY

you're DOING great

my PROGRESS IS RECOGNIZED, ~~even~~ especially WHEN I CAN'T see IT FOR myself

I CRY,

even WHEN I THINK I'm NOT going To. (RUDE)

We uncover STUFF I'D RATHER LEAVE BURIED and use IT To HELP me grow

Fear SHame gUILT etc.

I Realize I am carrying someTHING I DON'T NEED & I LEAVE IT BEHIND

Types of Therapy Sessions I Have Had

THE "SORRY I USED aLL your TISSUES" SESSION

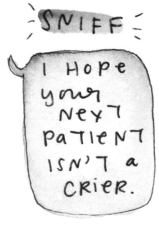

THE "OOPS, I ACCIDENTALLY OPENED THE FLOODGATES" SESSION

THE SESSION WHERE I UNEARTH a game-changing INSIGHT

THE SESSION I LEAVE FEELING HEAVIER

(SO MANY OF MY EARLY SESSIONS WERE LIKE THIS. I WOULD GIVE MYSELF PERMISSION TO TAKE THE REST OF THE DAY OFF, IF I COULD)

THE SESSION I leave FEELING LIGHTER

(HAPPENING MORE FREQUENTLY THESE DAYS)

WHEN I STARTED THERAPY, I THOUGHT IT WAS GOING TO FIX ALL MY ISSUES
CONGRATULATIONS! YOU ARE NOW PERFECTLY MENTALLY HEALTHY!

BUT THE LONGER I've gone,
THE more I've realized
IT'S NOT
aBout FIXING
ANYTHING

Because I'm NOT a BROKEN PERSON WHO NEEDS TO BE FIXED or a BAD PERSON WHO NEEDS TO BE CHANGED or a WRONG PERSON WHO NEEDS TO BE RIGHTED.

I am a
WHOLE
person

WHO NEEDS TO BE
accepted.

AND THE PERSON WHO NEEDS TO ACCEPT me IS me.

AND THAT'S WHERE ALL THE WORK OF THERAPY HAS BEEN.

IN THERAPY, I FOUND MYSELF IN THE SAFEST OF SAFE SPACES. MY THERAPIST SAW ME FULLY AND ACCEPTED ME COMPLETELY (REALLY! NO MATTER WHAT I TOLD HER!!)

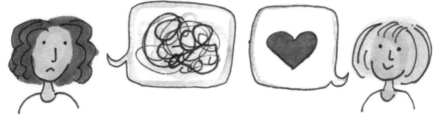

so THaT maybe
I COuLD LeaRN
To see myseLF
DIFFereNTLY

you're NOT
as BaD as
I THOughT

BECAUSE THE TRUTH IS: EVERYONE HAS THINGS ABOUT THEMSELVES THAT THEY DON'T LIKE

OUR ISSUES DON'T make us ANY LESS WHOLE, any LESS ENOUGH. ON THE CONTRARY, THEY make us more WONDERFULLY HUMAN maybe growing as a person — maybe healing — isn't about making the things you don't like about yourself miraculously disappear.

POOF!

UNWANTED TRAITS BE GONE!

maybe IT'S aBouT
meeTINg yourseLF
wHere you aLreaDy are.
IMPeRFecT, yes—
BuT
ENouGH.

I'm Having a HARD Time accepting you RIGHT NOW.
DON'T WORRY. I'LL Be Here FOR you WHEN you're Ready.

EVEN IF YOU'RE NOT **EXACTLY** WHERE you WANT TO BE

IT'S OKAY TO BE **WHEREVER** you are.

I used to think there was only

ONE RIGHT

way of being

Conform to expectations

Be perfect

"Have it all"

Don't disappoint anyone

Smile

and life was like keeping
to a very narrow
path

I was not allowed
to stray from

Fear,
Isolation,
Rejection,
&
Failure
constantly closing
in on me from all sides

AND THE OLDER I
GOT, THE NARROWER
THE PATH BECAME
UNTIL I COULD
BARELY
EVEN
BREATHE

BUT THEN ONE DAY
I LEARNED
THERE ARE MANY
WAYS OF BEING
NONE RIGHT
NONE WRONG
JUST DIFFERENT.

AND SUDDENLY LIFE WAS LIKE WANDERING IN THE DESERT

FLOATING IN the ocean

BEING caught IN THE curl OF a waVe

IT'S NOT THAT LIFE IS PERFECT HERE.
FAILURE & REJECTION,
FEAR & ISOLATION
STILL EXIST, STILL POSE
A RISK.

(THEY ARE PART OF THE EXPERIENCE.)

(SORRY.)

BUT THEY NO LONGER DEFINE THE SPACE

and Having a
LITTLe space
makes IT easier To
remember...

IT'S OKAY IF
WHAT YOU'RE DOING
IN LIFE
IS FIGURING OUT
WHAT YOU'RE
DOING IN LIFE

giving to **others**

but neglecting *yourself*

PRACTICING
SELF-CARE

and finding
you have

more & more to give

IT'S HARD TO grow.

you FIRST must
REALIZE you

CaN

WHICH IS HARDER THAN
you THINK,
especially
IF you've ONLY KNOWN
ONE way of BEING

THEN YOU HAVE TO
VENTURE OUT
INTO THE great
UNKNOWN

THOUGH YOU are STILL SO
TENDER AND FRAGILE

AND DO SOMETHING DIFFERENT FROM ANY—
THING YOU'VE DONE BEFORE

You HAVE TO PERSIST, REMEMBERING THAT

THE BAD IS HERE TO HELP, JUST AS MUCH AS THE GOOD

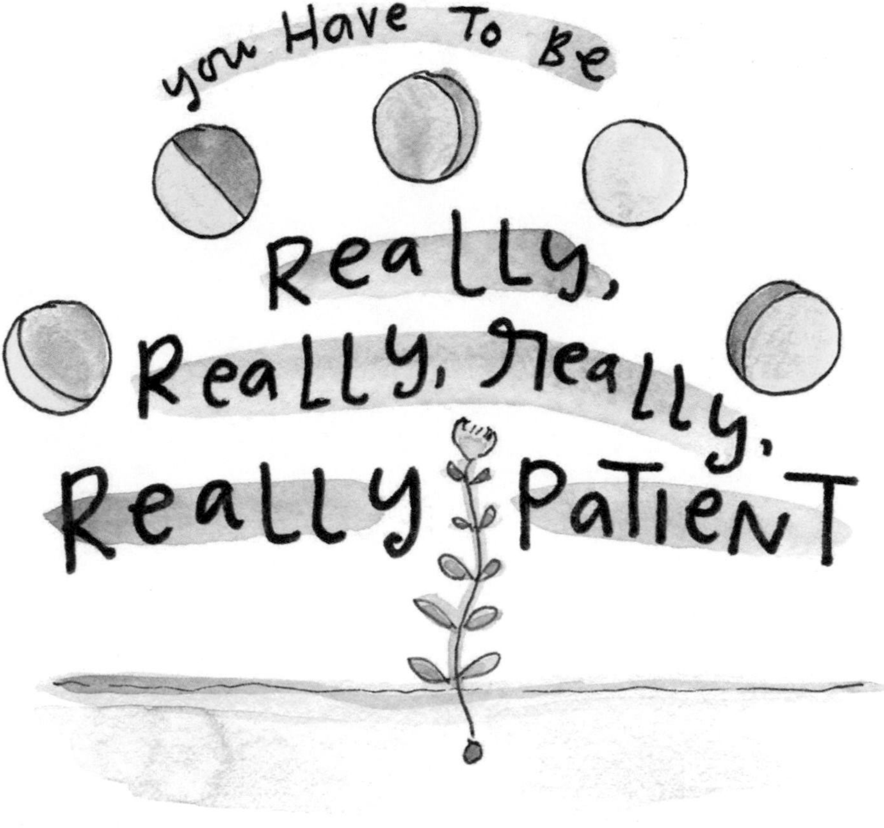
you have to be
really,
really, really, really,
really patient

BuT

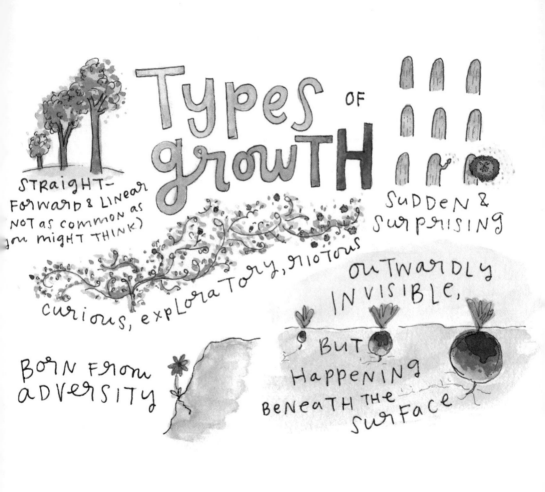

Types of growth

STRAIGHT-FORWARD & LINEAR (NOT as common as you might THINK)

SUDDEN & SURPRISING

curious, exploraTory, riotous

OUTWARDLY INVISIBLE, BUT HAPPENING BENEATH THE SURFACE

BORN FROM ADVERSITY

maybe SELF-LOVE IS NOT a goal To achieve, an END-POINT ON THE JOURNEY

maybe IT IS NOT a FEELING, BUT a CONSISTENT ACT. a CHOICE.

maybe LOVING yourself
DOESN'T MEAN always
FEELING WONDERFUL
aBOUT yourseLF
all THE Time

WE'Re
always Happy!

maybe SELF-LOVE
IS as Simple as making
KIND & LOVING CHOICES
FOR yourself.

maybe you Love
yourself if
you Take Care
of yourself

IF you say NO WHEN
you NEED TO *IT'S NOT THE RIGHT FIT*

IF you FORGIVE
yourself

IF you SPEAK KINDLY
TO yourself

IF you HONOR your NEEDS

IF you DO SOMETHING
you LOVE

IF you STAND UP
For yourseLF

IF you give yourseLF
NEW experiences
(EVEN IF THEY'RE NOT SO PLEASANT)

IF you ACKNOWLEDGE THAT THE JOURNEY IS LONG, AND WHEREVER you are ON IT IS OKAY

These are ALL ways of CHOOSING to SHOW yourself LOVE

mayBe you DON'T always FEEL LIKE you Really Love yourseLF. mayBe THAT's OKay. mayBe THE FacT THaT you are HeRe, STRIVING, **WORKING, TRYING** is a SIGN you <u>DO</u>.

NOW I FEEL LIKE
IT'S TIME TO TELL a
Wrap-up Story
TO END
THIS BOOK
ON a POSITIVE NOTE
AND TELL you HOW
I WON IN THE END.

How all the work I've done on myself has totally paid off, how I love and accept myself completely.

BUT THIS IS NOT THAT KIND OF STORY.

THE TRUTH IS, I STILL STRUGGLE WITH THIS STUFF EVERY SINGLE DAY.

WHAT IF IT'S SO STUPID?
WHAT IF IT makes me look super NEUROTIC? WHAT IF everyone HATES IT?
I WANTED THIS!
WHY CAN'T I ENJOY DOING IT?

ONE AFTERNOON, CLOSE TO MY PUBLISHER'S DEADLINE, I SAT ACROSS FROM MY THERAPIST AND DEMANDED:

AND MY THERAPIST REPLIED:

THE STORY ISN'T

~~SHE overcame ALL HER problems~~

~~SHE FIXED EVERYTHING~~

~~SHE LIVED HAPPILY EVER AFTER~~

SHE CHIPPED away aT HERSELF, LAYER BY Layer

SHONE a LIGHT INTO HER DARKEST PLACES, AND SAID TO EVERYTHING SHE FOUND:

THE STORY,
my THERAPIST SAID,
IS THAT IT'S POSSIBLE TO HAVE ALL THESE STRUGGLES AND TO CREATE SOMETHING IN SPITE OF THEM

To catch a glimpse of yourself, even just for a moment, as the powerful, magical, wondrous, astounding being that you are.

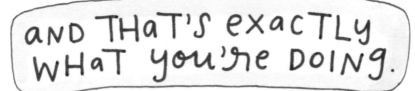

WELL...
PROBABLY.

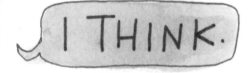

I THINK.

ABOUT THE AUTHOR

TORI PRESS IS AN ARTIST AND WRITER AND HIGHLY ANXIOUS HUMAN. BORN IN ATLANTA, GEORGIA, SHE SPENT 10 YEARS AS A GRAPHIC DESIGNER BEFORE QUITTING TO CREATE SPACE IN HER LIFE.

DRAWING CARTOONS WAS WHAT CAME IN TO FILL IT.

SHE LIVES IN LOS ANGELES, CALIFORNIA, WITH HER HUSBAND, TWO DAUGHTERS, DOG, AND APPROXIMATELY 57 HOUSEPLANTS.